W9-AEC-608

A scene from the Manhattan Theatre Club production of *Corpus Christi*. Set design by Loy Arcenas.

Photo by Joan Marcus

CORPUS CHRISTI

BY TERRENCE McNALLY

★

★

DRAMATISTS
PLAY SERVICE
INC.

CORPUS CHRISTI

Copyright © 1999, Terrence McNally

ALL RIGHTS RESERVED

CAUTION: Professionals and amateurs are hereby warned that performance of CORPUS CHRISTI is subject to a royalty. It is fully protected under the copyright laws of the United States of America, and of all countries covered by the International Copyright Union (including the Dominion of Canada and the rest of the British Commonwealth), and of all countries covered by the Pan-American Copyright Convention and the Universal Copyright Convention, the Berne Convention, and of all countries with which the United States has reciprocal copyright relations. All rights, including professional/amateur stage rights, motion picture, recitation, lecturing, public reading, radio broadcasting, television, video or sound recording, all other forms of mechanical or electronic reproduction, such as CD-ROM, CD-I, DVD, information storage and retrieval systems and photocopying, and the rights of translation into foreign languages, are strictly reserved. Particular emphasis is placed upon the question of readings, permission for which must be secured from the Author's agent in writing.

The English language stock and amateur stage performance rights in the United States, its territories, possessions and Canada in CORPUS CHRISTI are controlled exclusively by the DRAMATISTS PLAY SERVICE, INC., 440 Park Avenue South, New York, N.Y. 10016. No professional or non-professional performance of the Play may be given without obtaining in advance the written permission of the DRAMATISTS PLAY SERVICE, INC., and paying the requisite fee.

Inquiries concerning all other rights should be addressed to William Morris Agency, Inc., 1325 Avenue of the Americas, New York, N.Y. 10019, Attn: Gilbert Parker.

SPECIAL NOTE

Anyone receiving permission to produce CORPUS CHRISTI is required to (1) give credit to the Author as sole and exclusive Author of the Play on the title page of all programs distributed in connection with performances of the Play and in all instances in which the title of the Play appears for purposes of advertising, publicizing or otherwise exploiting the Play and/or a production thereof. The name of the Author must appear on a separate line, in which no other name appears, immediately beneath the title and in size of type equal to 50% of the size of the largest most prominent letter used for the title of the Play. No person, firm or entity may receive credit larger or more prominent that that accorded the Author; and (2) to give the following acknowledgment on the title page in all programs distributed in connection with performances of the Play:

Originally produced by the Manhattan Theatre Club on September 22, 1998.

SPECIAL NOTE ON SONGS AND RECORDINGS

For performance of the songs, arrangements and recordings mentioned in this Play that are protected by copyright, the permission of the copyright owners must be obtained; or other songs, arrangements and recordings in the public domain substituted.

2

CORPUS CHRISTI is dedicated to my partner

GARY BONASORTE

The author would like to thank the North Carolina School of the Arts for its support in the development of CORPUS CHRISTI.

CORPUS CHRISTI received its world premiere at Manhattan Theatre Club (Lynne Meadow, Artistic Director; Barry Grove, Managing Director) in New York City, on September 22, 1998. It was directed by Joe Mantello; the set design was by Loy Arcenas; the costume design was by Jess Goldstein; the lighting design was by Brian MacDevitt; the original music and arrangements were by Drew McVety; the sound design was by David van Tieghem; and the production stage manager was James Fitzsimmons. The cast was as follows:

JAMES, ET AL.	Sean Dugan
THOMAS, ET AL.	Christopher Fitzgerald
PETER, ET AL.	Michael Hall
JOHN, ET AL.	Michael Irby
JAMES THE LESS, ET AL.	Ken Leung
JUDAS	Josh Lucas
PHILIP, ET AL.	Matthew Mabe
MATTHEW, ET AL.	Drew McVety
JOSHUA	Anson Mount
BARTHOLOMEW, ET AL.	Jeremy Shamos
SIMON, ET AL.	Ben Sheaffer
THADDEUS, ET AL.	Troy Sostillio
ANDREW, ET AL.	Greg Zola

THE CAST

The play has been written to be performed by a company of 13 actors, all male. One actor will play the role of JOSHUA; another the role of JUDAS. The 11 other actors will play a variety of roles. The distribution of these roles will be at the discretion of the director.

THE SETTING

The play has been written with a bare raked stage in mind. Members of the company will sit on benches at the rear of the stage when they are not participating in a scene. Thus, an "entrance" is a simple stepping forward, while an "exit" is only a turning away and returning to the company bench. While seated, the actors observe the scene in progress and may even comment on it, either to the actors in the scene, among themselves or to the audience.

Two design elements are important: a small pool of water and a perpetual fire, both in the floor of the stage.

CHARACTERS

JOSHUA
JOHN — a writer, brother to James
JAMES — a teacher
PETER — a young man who sells fish
ANDREW — a masseur
PHILIP — a hustler
BARTHOLOMEW — a doctor and James' lover
JUDAS ISCARIOT — a restauranteur
MATTHEW — a lawyer
THOMAS — an actor
JAMES THE LESS — an architect
SIMON — a singer
THADDEUS — a hairdresser

"KOSTYA *(Looking round the stage.)* There's a theatre for you! Just a curtain, two wings, and then open space. Not a bit of scenery. A view straight onto the lake and the far horizon. We'll raise the curtain at half past eight, exactly, when the moon rises."

Anton Chekhov. *The Seagull.* Act One

CORPUS CHRISTI

The house lights are still up as the Actors begin to drift on stage. They are wearing street clothes. They may either talk among themselves, greet people in the audience or quietly prepare for the performance. Some of them will check the prop tables which are visible stage right and left. The mood is informal, lightly bantering, loving even.

The play itself "begins" when from off-stage we hear the three loud, deliberate knocks of a wooden staff forcefully striking the stage floor. At once the Actors are silent and gather in a more formal grouping.

Again, the three knocks from off-stage. One of the Actors steps forward.

ACTOR. We are going to tell you an old and familiar story. One you've all heard over and over, again and again. One you believe or one you don't. There's no suspense and fewer surprises. You all know how it turns out. But it's a story that bears repeating. Some say it can't be told enough. The playwright asks your indulgence, as do we, the actors. There are no tricks up our sleeves. No malice in our hearts. We're glad you're here. *(The house lights are lowered. One of the Actors begins to sing (a capella) "Were You There When They Crucified My Lord?"* The other Actors join in as they begin to undress and change into the "uniform" of the play: white shirt, khaki trousers and bare feet. The Actor Playing John cups his hands together while the Actor Playing Peter fills them with water from a pitcher. One by one, the other Actors will pass in front of the Actor Playing John who raises his cupped hands over them and lets the water run down their bared heads.)*

---

*See Special Note on Songs and Recordings on copyright page.

JOHN. I bless you, *(full name of the Actor Playing Andrew)*. I baptize you and recognize your divinity as a human being. I adore you, *(first name of the Actor Playing Andrew)*. I christen you Andrew.

ANDREW. Andrew's hands were his livelihood. He was a masseur. He didn't say much when he worked. He didn't figure he had to. Already I've said more. If he liked you, you knew it. If he didn't like you, you really knew it. And if he loved you! Bliss. Andrew loved Joshua. That was our name for Him. He loved Joshua a lot. *(He turns away and continues to dress as the Actor Playing James steps forward and kneels before the Actor Playing John. This same ritual will continue until all 11 other Actors are baptized. After he is so blessed and has introduced himself, each Actor will finish changing into his plain white shirt and crisp pair of khakis while remaining barefoot. Now John baptizes the Actor Playing James.)*

JOHN. I bless you, *(full name of the Actor Playing James)*. I baptize you and recognize your divinity as a human being. I adore you, *(first name of the Actor Playing James)*. I christen you James.

JAMES. I'm a teacher. High school. It's a tough age. I teach history, world history. They hate it. I don't care. I love what I do. What happened and why. How we learn from it or we don't. Cool. Very cool. I love my sandwich and apple in a brown paper bag. I love chalk and blackboards and erasers and maps you pull down of the Roman Empire. I can see where I am on it. This little dot, Corpus Christi, and I'm there. I love that. *(He turns away as the Actor Playing Bartholomew steps forward)*

JOHN. I bless you, *(full name of the Actor Playing Bartholomew)*. I baptize you and recognize your divinity as a human being. I adore you, *(first name of the Actor Playing Bartholomew)*. I christen you Bartholomew.

BARTHOLOMEW. I hope that's not the same water we used the last performance. Laugh, but Bartholomew was a doctor. That's exactly the kind of thing he'd be worried about. We have to heal men's bodies before we can heal their souls. Joshua didn't always understand that. "Believe," He'd say, "believe and be well." I'd be right behind Him saying "Believe and take two of these and call me in the morning."

JOHN. I bless you, *(full name of the Actor Playing Simon)*. I baptize you and recognize your divinity as a human being. I adore you, *(first name of the Actor Playing Simon)*. I christen you Simon.

SIMON. Thank you. I love being Simon. Simon was a singer. Well, among other things he was a singer. First and foremost he was a disciple, a follower of Joshua. I don't know why following has such a bad name. With the right leader, with the right guys, it can be wonderful. All my life I wanted to belong to something and here I was, right smack in the middle. I hope you're as fortunate. I know this much: Before I had to sing to be happy. Now I sing because I am happy. I'm singing all the time.

JOHN. I bless you, *(full name of the Actor Playing Matthew)*. I baptize you and recognize your divinity as a human being. I adore you, *(first name of the Actor Playing Matthew)*. I christen you Matthew.

MATTHEW. Matthew was a lawyer, a brilliant one. The kind they write novels about. He had it all: a corner office, a drop-dead apartment, a good car, a house at the beach. He was made a full partner at 31. Are you impressed? He was. We had a lot to get over. I believe it's called attitude. The first time I met Joshua I didn't like Him. I'd worked very hard to get this much of a piece of the pie — a lot of us had — (my father delivered mail!) and here He was saying I had to give it all away. It pissed me off. He still does sometimes but hey, I'm learning to be a team player, you know? It's not easy. I had a corner office.

JOHN. I bless you, *(full name of the Actor Playing Thomas)*. I baptize you and recognize your divinity as a human being. I adore you, *(first name of the Actor Playing Thomas)*. I christen you Thomas.

THOMAS. I'm an actor. I mean Thomas is an actor. I'm an actor, too, of course, but you know that or you wouldn't be paying good money or even no money to sit there and listen to me tell you I'm someone else, in this case the ever popular and appealing Thomas. It's called the willing suspension of disbelief — or in certain cases the *un*willing suspension of disbelief. I've seen audiences fight a play for an entire performance. At the end of the evening, they're exhausted. So are we. I bet even the ushers and the stagehands are feeling the fatigue. Why do that to yourself? Or us? We want to take you someplace beautiful, someplace thrilling, someplace maybe you've never been before.

11

Come with us. At least meet us halfway. I think you'll like Thomas. I know I do. We're both 25. We never get the girl. Or the guy. We're both character actors which is short for short and not looking like some of these other bimbos. I'm going to play the shit out of this part.

JOHN. I bless you, *(full name of the Actor Playing James The Less)*. I baptize you and recognize your divinity as a human being. I adore you, *(first name of the Actor Playing James The Less)*. I christen you James The Less.

JAMES THE LESS. Hell of a name to stick someone with but it was in fact what Joshua called me when it turned out He already had a James. I didn't take it personally, he lied. This James, James the Less, was an architect. He had a profound sense of order, a subtle intuition for volume, almost a child's delight in the play of light and shadow and a passionate commitment to function. What he designed had to work, it had to do something. Otherwise, why make it? I designed the Roman cross I'm ashamed to say. At the time, I thought nothing of it. The perfect killing machine, they called it. An idiot could have thought of it. If you do this to someone, *(He holds his arms out.)* — after a while their lungs implode and they suffocate. I hate the Romans.

JOHN. I bless you, *(full name of the Actor Playing Thaddeus)*. I baptize you and recognize your divinity as a human being. I adore you, *(first name of the Actor Playing Thaddeus)*. I christen you Thaddeus.

THADDEUS. Thaddeus was a hairdresser. Does anybody have a problem with that? Good.

JOHN. I bless you, *(full name of the Actor Playing Philip)*. I baptize you and recognize your divinity as a human being. I adore you, *(first name of the Actor Playing Philip)*. I christen you Philip.

PHILIP. They don't know much about me. I like that. This much is certain: He was probably Greek. His father was an apothecary. He was in his early thirties when he met Joshua and the others. They have no idea how old he was when he died or how. And that's all, folks. They don't know anything else about him. He's not one of those people who leave a record. I like being Philip. I can be anyone I want to be. Except Him. I could never be Him.

MATTHEW. You didn't tell them you were a hustler.

PHILIP. It must have slipped my mind.

SIMON. Give it a rest, Matthew.

THE ACTOR PLAYING PETER. Excuse me, do you think we could do me now?

JOHN. I'm sorry, of course. I bless you, *(full name of the Actor Playing Simon Peter).*

THE ACTOR PLAYING PETER. That's better already.

JOHN. I baptize you and recognize your divinity as a human being. I adore you, *(first name of the Actor Playing Simon Peter).* I christen you Peter.

PETER. Peter, Simon Peter is probably the most familiar of us to you. Well, after Joshua, of course. And I suppose Judas Iscariot. And John the Baptist, I guess. Let me start again. Peter, Simon Peter is probably the fourth most familiar of us to you. He was a fisherman. Nothing made him happier than to come home with his nets bulging with fish he'd pulled from the sea with his own two hands. Tuna, red snapper, cod. The occasional eel. He loved that flopping sound they made on his deck. There'd be good eating tonight. The first time I saw Joshua it took my breath away. I forgot all about my fish. Half of them flopped right back into the sea. I didn't care. *(Two Actors remain. The others have formed a half-circle around them.)*

JOHN. One of you must be Him.

THE ACTOR PLAYING JOSHUA. Is it I?

THE ACTOR PLAYING JUDAS. Is it I?

JOHN. You know who it is. Accept it. *(One of the two Actors stands up/comes forward.)*

THE ACTOR PLAYING JOSHUA. It is I.

JOHN. I bless you, *(full name of the Actor Playing Joshua).* I baptize you and recognize your divinity as a human being. I love you, *(first name of the Actor Playing Joshua).* I christen you Jesus, son of Mary and Joseph, Son of God, son of man. *(The Actor howls as if scalded as the water is poured over him.)* I christen you Joshua. *(The Actor has stopped howling.)* I've been waiting for You.

THADDEUS. We all have. *(He takes John's place as the Actor Playing John kneels while Joshua blesses and baptizes him, Thaddeus helping with the pitcher of water.)*

JOSHUA. I bless you, *(full name of the Actor Playing John)*. I baptize you and recognize your divinity as a human being. I adore you, *(first name of the Actor Playing John)*. I christen you John, my cousin. *(Thaddeus and Matthew bring Joshua and John their white shirts and khakis. They begin to dress.)*

JOHN. I was lucky. I was born with faith. I knew You would come.

JOSHUA. How did you know it was Me when even I didn't.

JOHN. There was a halo around Your head, coz.

JOSHUA. Be serious!

JOHN. I am. You're the only one who didn't see it. Are we all here then? *(One Actor has remained alone and apart from the others.)*

THE ACTOR PLAYING JUDAS. What about me?

JOSHUA. Come. *(Joshua motions the Actor forward. The Actor Playing Judas kneels before Joshua for his blessing and baptism but he does not bow his head. Instead he looks right at Joshua.)*

JUDAS. So here we are again.

JOSHUA. I bless you, *(full name of the Actor Playing Judas)*. I baptize you and recognize your divinity as a human being. *(The Actor shudders as the water is poured over him.)* I adore you, *(first name of the Actor Playing Judas)*. I christen you Judas. *(The Actor Playing Judas stops shuddering and looks up at Joshua.)* I did love you, you know.

JUDAS. Not the way I wanted. *(The other Actors line the stage apron, impatient to begin.)* Judas Iscariot, Scorpio. November 6TH. You figure the year. I'm smart. I like to read. I like music. Good music. I like the theatre. Good theatre. I like some sports. I like violence. I take good care of myself. Weak bodies disgust me. I've got a big dick. *(There are razzes from the ranks.)* It's important. It's important to me. Everybody is going to tell the truth about himself this time! Even Joshua.

JOSHUA. Especially Joshua.

JAMES. Get on with it, Judas.

JUDAS. No one has ever told this story right. Even when they get the facts right, the feeling is wrong. One and one are two.

So what? What does that tell you about anything? This is what matters. *(He hits his right hand into his chest.)* The only thing. Nothing else. *(More razzes. Judas will continue over them.)* People can't stand the truth. They want their Joshua, seen through their eyes, told through their lies. Truth is brutal. It scalds, it stings. *(Judas is being shouted down by the others. Simon and Philip have gone to the prop table and picked up a large basket filled with folded slips of paper. They will pass in front of the others who will draw five or six slips apiece. On these folded slips of paper are written the names of the other "roles" they will play in the story that follows.)*

SIMON.   We need a cast of thousands to tell this story: men, women, children.

JAMES THE LESS.   None of us knows who he's going to be.

PHILIP.   It's the luck of the draw.

BARTHOLOMEW.   A Roman centurion.

THADDEUS.   I'll trade you for Peggy Powell.

THOMAS.   Lazarus! Finally. Something I can get my teeth into.

JAMES.   Much scenery will be chewed at this performance!

THOMAS.   It's a very emotional story. So I'm not a minimalist.

JOHN.   Does everybody know who they are? All right, props! *(One by one various props are displayed to the audience and then returned to their place on the prop tables or in the wings.)*

ANDREW.   Nails. More like small spikes actually. Jesus, look at these things!

PHILIP.   A hammer to drive the nails.

JOHN.   Thirty pieces of silver and a noose.

THOMAS.   A loaf of bread.

THADDEUS.   Rope. For He was bound to a pillar and scourged.

JAMES THE LESS.   The scourge.

MATTHEW.   A crown of thorns.

SIMON.   His mother's Grand Ol' Opry souvenir ashtray.

PETER.   I'll take that, thank you.

THOMAS.   A fish. *(He holds up a fresh fish.)* Pee-eew!

BARTHOLOMEW.   Vinegar.

ANDREW.   Sponge.

THADDEUS.   The spear that pierced His side to end us His dreadful suffering.

PETER.   The chalice.

SIMON.   His little dog, Nebuchadnezzar. *(The dog is a stuffed animal on wheels that is easily pulled behind you.)*

JAMES THE LESS.   *(To us.)* I bet you didn't know about the little dog.

MATTHEW.   *(The same.)* Every kid has a dog. *(We can hear the sound of hammering from off-stage. When it is not actually heard during a silence or pause, it will be subliminal. We must never forget it. John has gone to Joshua and put his arm around him.)*

PETER.   A pair of blue suede shoes.

SIMON.   A pink suede belt.

JAMES.   A high school varsity letter.

THOMAS.   Cool.

MATTHEW.   For what sport?

JOSHUA.   Speech and drama.

MATTHEW.   Not cool. A picture of James Dean.

JOSHUA.   Let them see it. *(Matthew gives the picture to someone in the first row.)*

MATTHEW.   Pass it around, will you? Thanks.

PETER.   A pack of Lucky Strike cigarettes, their stubs carefully snuffed out in a Maxwell House coffee can kept hidden under His bed along with the picture of James Dean.

JAMES.   A copy of the Old Testament. The new one hasn't been written yet.

BARTHOLOMEW.   His diary. No one knew He kept one. *(Judas, sitting on one of the benches, staying apart from the others.)*

JUDAS.   I did.

BARTHOLOMEW.   Anyway it was lost. Imagine if it hadn't been.

JAMES.   We wouldn't be doing this.

JOSHUA.   The cross? What about the cross?

JOHN.   They're making it. *(He nods off-stage.)* Hear them? *(The hammering will continue.)*

JOSHUA.   No.

JOHN.   That's because You don't want to hear them. Are we ready then? Scene One. The nativity. *(John is a great stage manager. When he claps his hands, people jump to it. The stage is a swirl of activity as the Actors set up for the next scene. The Actors not in the scene sit on the benches at the rear of stage and watch. They may occasionally comment on the scene that follows. They definitely supply appropriate sound effects.)*

"Away in a manger
No crib for his bed

O little town of Bethlehem
How still we see thee lie

Jingle bells, jingle bells
Jingle all the way"*

(A TV is blaring. A football game is in progress. A Motel Manager is showing a vacant room to Peter/Mary, mother of Joshua, whose abdomen bulges as if pregnant.)

BARTHOLOMEW/MOTEL MANAGER. It's a big football weekend. This is the best we have. Take it or leave it, lady.

MARY. It's fine.

MOTEL MANAGER. Where's your uh husband?

MARY. Unloading the car.

MOTEL MANAGER. How soon are you going to, you know, pop?

MARY. I think right now. *(Mary gives birth and takes a doll out from under her skirt.)*

MOTEL MANAGER. Jesus Christ. What is it?

MARY. A boy.

MOTEL MANAGER. That's good. I like boys. Boys are best. The ice machine is outside to your left. *(At a cheer from the TV.)* They scored again! I fucking don't believe it. *(To Mary who has begun to nurse.)* Hey, you're not going to try anything funny with that kid. You know, stuff him down the crapper or something. Don't laugh. It wouldn't be the first. That's the last fucking thing I need this weekend: an infantesticide ... *(He has trouble with such a long word.)* ... that's what they call 'em! *(He goes. One of the Actors begins to play "Ave Maria"* on the violin. If no one in the cast can play "Ave Maria"* on the violin, one of them should pantomime it to recorded music. The Actor will enter the playing area of the motel scene but be invisible to the participants. Mary cradles the doll in her arm as*

---

*See Special Note on Songs and Recordings on copyright page.

17

Joshua makes gurgling, crying "baby" sounds appropriate for a newborn infant.)

MARY.   Ssssh, ssshh, it's all right. Mommy's here. *(Mary sings a song of the period. *)*

JOSHUA.   I was so cute! Look at Me! Where did all the blonde hair come from? *(We hear sounds of a couple making wild, uninhibited love in the room next door.)*

MARY.   Such a beautiful child He is. Perfect limbs. Perfect features.

JOSHUA.   And you were so pretty! Look how pretty my mom was, everyone. Like someone in the movies!

WOMAN NEXT DOOR/JAMES.   Fuck me, fuck me, fuck me.

MAN NEXT DOOR/ANDREW.   That's what I'm doing, you damn woman. I'm fucking you, I'm fucking you, I'm fucking you. *(Philip gets up from his place on the bench and comes into the motel room. He is Joshua's father, Joseph.)*

JOSEPH.   Sounds like somebody's having some fun next door. Is that? So soon? It's big. I didn't think it would be so big. Can I hold it? Thank you. It's a boy. Hey, little fella. You gonna grow up and be an All-American halfback? *(To Mary.)* You look so beautiful, Mother. Radiant.

JOSHUA.   How they must have loved each other!

JOSEPH.   This isn't easy for me to say Mare, but I'm going to love Him like He's my own, even if He's not.

JOSHUA.   My father said that. My father loved me!

MARY.   He's not anyone else's. I swear on my life. I'm a virgin, Joe.

JOSEPH.   No one knows that more than I do.

MARY.   I don't know what's going on here anymore than you do.

JOSEPH.   What are we gonna tell people when I take you back home?

MARY.   It's none of their damn business. And I'm not saying He's adopted!

JOSEPH.   What are we gonna call Him?

MARY.   I told you. Jesus.

JOSEPH.   I told you no. This is Texas. It sounds like a Mexican.

MARY.   I love Him so much already. Don't judge us too harshly,

---

*See Special Note on Songs and Recordings on copyright page.

18

Son. *(Simon, Thaddeus and Thomas begin singing.)*

"We three kings of orient are.
Bearing gifts we travel afar"*

Oh, listen, they're singing! I love Christmas. *(The three enter the room together.)*

SIMON/ROOM SERVICE #1.   Room service!

JOSEPH.   We didn't order.

ROOM SERVICE #1.   It's on the house. We heard something very special was happening in room 37 tonight.

JOSEPH.   Something very special has.

THADDEUS/ROOM SERVICE #2.   I hope you like Cuban cigars, Dad. Congratulations.

JOSEPH.   Why thank you kindly.

THOMAS/ROOM SERVICE #3.   I know you didn't order this but every boy wants a Flexible Flyer when he grows up.

JOSEPH.   We're from South Texas, mister. It hasn't snowed in Corpus Christi since the last time Hell froze over, which is never, if you catch my drift.

JOSHUA.   Thank you anyway. *(It begins to snow.)* Look, everybody!

JOSEPH.   Jesus Christ, Mary!

MARY.   It's a miracle.

JOSHUA.   It's not a miracle. It's snow.

ROOM SERVICE #3.   What's Your name, little tiger?

JOSHUA.   They haven't given Me one yet.

ROOM SERVICE #3.   You're going to save the world no matter what they call You. Beowulf, Charlemagne, Lucille Ball. What's in a name? It's who You are, what You do that matters.

JOSHUA.   Thank you, sir.

ROOM SERVICE #1.   Are you the mother? We have tidings for the mother, too.

JOSEPH.   Doesn't she look wonderful for a woman who's just given birth to a very large child, gentlemen?

ROOM SERVICE #1.   Hail, Mary, full of grace. The Lord is with thee.

MARY.   Well, I don't know about that but thank you kindly.

*See Special Note on Songs and Recordings on copyright page.

19

ROOM SERVICE #2.   Blessed is the fruit of thy womb, Jesus.

MARY.   We decided to call him Joshua actually.

ROOM SERVICE #1.   We bear you tidings: this is the child the world has waited for.

ROOM SERVICE #2.   He will die for our sins: mine and yours.

ROOM SERVICE #3.   His love for the world will redeem us all.

MARY.   So you're telling me He's a special child?

ROOM SERVICE #1.   We're telling you this child is the Son of God.

MARY.   Hell, every mother feels that way.

ROOM SERVICE #1.   Cherish and love Him.

MARY.   What does it look like I'm doing? You have some kid chewing on your tits and see how you like it. And I don't need a bunch a strangers telling me I don't know how to raise my own child.

JOSEPH.   She's just a little testy.

MARY.   I'm not testy, I'm sore. I wish everybody would get out of here.

JOSEPH.   We got a long drive tomorrow. Thanks for the presents and the good wishes, gentlemen. Happy holidays. *(Thomas, Thaddeus and Simon return to the bench, singing "We Three Kings of Orient Are"* as they go.)* Hey, it's Christmas. Are we gonna drink us a couple o' tequila sunrises and do us a little jukin' or what? Elvis has a new hit out.

MARY.   What if my child needs me?

JOSEPH.   I'll tell you who needs you: I do. I have needs. Now, I'll give you fifteen seconds, Mare. Not thirty. Not twenty. Fifteen. You got that?

MARY.   Got it. (Die.) *(Joseph goes back to the bench.)* You look like You're trying to say something. That's all I need: a kid who starts talking early, like I don't have enough of a headache. Who are You? Where did You come from? I know You're not really mine.

JOSHUA.   Sshh, sshh, you don't have to talk. Just hold Me.

JOSEPH.   Mary!

MARY.   If You're the Son of God, what does that make me?

JOSHUA.   The mother of the Son of God.

MARY.   I don't know if I can do this.

---

*See Special Note on Songs and Recordings on copyright page.

JOSHUA. Sure you can. It's easy. You're doing great.

JOSEPH. Goddamnit, Mary!

JOSHUA. Leave us alone!

JOSEPH. One!

MARY. So little!

JOSHUA. I'm sorry. I'll grow. I promise.

JOSEPH. Two!

MARY. So unprotected!

JOSHUA. That's okay. I have you.

JOSEPH. Three!

JOSHUA. Don't go.

MARY. I'm sorry. He's calling me.

JOSEPH. Goddamnit it all to hell!

MARY. Coming! (*She goes. Joshua stands looking down at the doll and makes baby sounds again. And now we hear the sounds of a terrible fight coming from the room on the other side of Joshua's.*)

ANGRY MAN/JOHN. You stupid piece of shit. You fucking cow.

FRIGHTENED WOMAN/MATTHEW. I'm sorry. Just don't hit me again.

ANGRY MAN. Just don't (*Sounds of a hit.*) you again? Is that what you said? Just don't fucking (*Sounds of a hit.*) hit you again? Is that what you (*Sounds of a hit, sounds of a hit, sounds of a hit.*) fucking said to me? (*Silence. We hear only Joshua's baby sounds.*) Now what? You just gonna lie there like that? Fuck this shit. (*Sounds of a door slamming.*)

JAMES THE LESS/GOD. Joshua. Joshua. Joshua. This is the Lord God, Your father. Stop crying and be a man. Much has been given to You because much is expected of You. Men are cruel. They are not happy. They sicken and die and turn away from love. I want You to show them there is another way. The way of love and generosity and self peace. You will comfort a woman who lies battered in a motel room next to Yours. You will forgive the man who left her there. You will teach a couple in another motel room that there is more to love than —

WOMAN NEXT DOOR/JAMES. Fuck me, fuck me, fuck me!

GOD. — but you will allow them that —

MAN NEXT DOOR/BARTHOLEMEW. I'm fucking you, I'm fucking you, I'm fucking you!

GOD. — has its pleasures, too. You will work miracles. You will demonstrate patience and practice inexorable determination. When You are much too young You will die a terrible death at the very hands of those I gave You to. Before then You will know suffering but You will also know laughter and friendship and the joy of skinny-dipping on a warm summer's day and the pleasure of a fine meal of roast lamb and fresh-baked bread washed down with a hearty red wine. Your name will still be spoken one thousand nine hundred and ninety eight years after Your birth.

JOSHUA. You said I will suffer?

GOD. Terribly. But You will know great joy as well.

JOSHUA. Why must I suffer?

GOD. Why not?

JOSHUA. Why Me?

GOD. Why not You? *(God whispers something in Joshua's ear.)*

JOSHUA. What? I couldn't hear You.

GOD. All men are divine.

JOSHUA. Why are You whispering?

GOD. That is the secret You will teach them.

JOSHUA. What if I don't want to share this secret with My fellow men?

GOD. You won't be able to keep it.

JOSHUA. What if I don't believe it Myself?

GOD. No more questions. I'm gone, Joshua.

JOSHUA. What do You mean, You're gone? You can't be gone. You're supposed to everywhere all the time.

GOD. That is a very big misunderstanding. *(Bartholomew crosses to Joshua.)*

BARTHOLOMEW. Give Him to me.

JOSHUA. What for?

BARTHOLOMEW. The circumcision.

THOMAS. Could we just skip this scene?

BARTHOLOMEW. Everybody's so squeamish.

MATTHEW/PRIEST. Why aren't You playing football?

JOSHUA. I don't want to.

PRIEST. What kind of answer is that, boy? Sure You do! Every boy in Corpus Christi plays football. *(The other Actors have begun to toss footballs back and forth, having fun.)* How old are You?

JOSHUA. 13.

PRIEST. 13? You're small for Your age. I thought You were ten. *(Calling to another boy.)* How old would you say this one looks?

BOY. Nine. He's in the wrong school!

PRIEST. They ought to get You some of them hormone shots. Let me see You throw a football. *(Joshua throws the ball.)* That's not how You throw a football. This is how You throw a football. Are You gonna cry on me?

JOSHUA. No, sir.

PRIEST. You like scouts?

JOSHUA. Yes, sir.

PRIEST. Good, we'll make a football player out of You. You like pussy? Pussy is girls. You like girls?

JOSHUA. Yes, sir. *(This time Joshua throws the ball with startling speed and accuracy, catching the Priest off-guard. The Priest throws it back to Joshua. The football goes back and forth with increasing hostility. Again the other boys stop to watch.)*

PRIEST. You got a girlfriend?

JOSHUA. No, sir.

PRIEST. Well then maybe You don't like girls

JOSHUA. Yes , sir.

PRIEST. You gonna say yes, sir, no, sir to every cotton-picking thing I say?

JOSHUA. I'm sorry, sir.

PRIEST. Sir-ring somebody like that don't sound polite. It sounds more like sass and nobody likes to be sassed. Especially an overworked, underpaid Roman Catholic priest who has to be a goddamn scout master after school. Don't You think I have better things to do with my time than try to teach You how to throw a football?

JOSHUA. Ow. You're hurting Me.

PRIEST. Well ain't that a goddamn shame.

THOMAS/SISTER JOSEPH. Leave the child alone Father McMullen. He's late for play practice.

PRIEST. Of course, Sister Joseph. We were just playing. See why we never get married, Josh? So some woman can't tell us what to do the rest of our life. *(He goes.)*

SISTER JOSEPH. There goes a man who doesn't like who he is. Are You all right?

JOSHUA. Yes, Sister. *(Sister Joseph goes to a piano. Joshua stands C.)*

SISTER JOSEPH. I hope You've been working on Your number. We open in two weeks. Now set the scene for Yourself. You're alone on a beautiful beach. You're in love. Have You ever been in love, Joshua?

JOSHUA. No, ma'am.

SISTER JOSEPH. Well, as I used to say before I took my holy vows, we'll just have to fake it. *(She plays an elaborate flourish.)* And ... *(Joshua and Sister Joseph sing a song from a Broadway musical of the period.*)* Who are You saving it for anyway? Seven, eight ... *(Joshua and Sister Joseph continue to sing.)*

MARY. You through with Him, sister?

SISTER JOSEPH. Show Your mother what we've been doing, Joshua.

MARY. I saw enough, thank you. Not quite my cup of tea. I'm driving Him to his ballroom dance class. They're teaching Him to hold a woman proper. I figure that's a little out of your milieu, sister.

SISTER JOSEPH. Ballroom dance class? They grow up so fast. He's a very special child.

MARY. I've been hearing that all his life. I'm still waiting.

JOSHUA. Good-bye, sister. I'll remember what you said.

MARY. What did she say?

JOSHUA. Nothing.

MARY. You start listening to nuns, You're going to get Yourself entirely screwed up. *(She holds up a 45RPM record. The violin music gets much livelier.)* Now who's little sixth-grader is ready to rock and roll with His ol' mama! *(Joshua tries to dance with Mary.)* No, darlin', put Your hands around me this way. The man leads the woman. Just listen to the music. It'll tell You what to do. I give up.

JOSHUA. Do you ever hear hammering?

---

*See Special Note on Songs and Recordings on copyright page.

24

MARY. You're father's a carpenter. Of course I hear hammering. What's the matter with You?

JOSHUA. I'm sorry.

MARY. You're not much of a dancer either. All those lessons!

JOSHUA. No, ma'am.

MARY. And I'm a woman who loves to dance.

JOSHUA. Yes, ma'am.

MARY. I told Your father: no wonder I go out nights. I'm just looking for someone who wants to dance with me. Hell, I even tried to turn You into a little Gene Kelly.

JOSHUA. Don't cry, ma'am.

MARY. I'm not crying. Why should I cry? And don't start that ma'am business with me, Joshua. We're both too old for it.

JOSHUA. I'm 17. I just look young for My age. So do you. You're still so beautiful.

MARY. You're a sweet boy, Joshua. Too bad You're not a dancer. We could have had some fun. *(Philip/Mrs. McElroy has begun to set up a chess board.)*

JOSHUA. There's Mrs. McElroy, I gotta go.

MARY. I'm not through with You. *(But Joshua has already joined Mrs. McElroy.)*

JOSHUA. I memorized another Shakespeare sonnet, Mrs. McElroy. "When to the."

MRS. McELROY. Slow down, Joshua, not so fast! *(The fiddler will begin to play the Meditation from Massenet's opera* Thais. *)*

MARY. What are you teaching Him at that public high school of yours, Mrs. McElroy?

JOSHUA. She's teaching Me that this town is the armpit of Western Civilization.

MRS. McELROY. Joshua!

JOSHUA. "When to the sessions of sweet silent thought."

MARY. 'Cause you're not teaching Him to dance.

JOSHUA. "I summon up remembrance of thing past."

MARY. You're not teaching Him to love and respect His own mother. I've got my eye on you. I know what you're doing. *(She goes back to the bench and sits.)*

---

*See Special Note on Songs and Recordings on copyright page.

MRS. McELROY. You're going to get me into trouble with Your folks. *(They begin to play chess.)*

JOSHUA. My mother doesn't like Me, Mrs. McElroy, and My father is never around.

MRS. McELROY. It's hard, I know. When I was Your age I ...

JOSHUA. What? Tell me!

MRS. McELROY. I've always found consolation in the master-pieces of English literature, especially the Romantic poets.

JOSHUA. What do you have to be consoled about? I'll console you.

MRS. McELROY. Your move, Joshua.

JOSHUA. What's that music? It's pretty.

MRS. McELROY. This particular selection is known as "The Meditation" from *Thais*, a French opera by one Jules Massenet.

JOSHUA. Jules Massenet.

MRS. McELROY. The eponymous heroine sits looking at her reflection in a mirror, meditating that her beauty, like all else, it, too, shall fade.

JOSHUA. I think you're beautiful. *(As the Actor who plays the fiddle rips into a lively dance tune, the other Actors erupt from the benches in a noisy phalanx of rootin', tootin' teenagers. Joshua continues with Mrs. McElroy. Only Judas remains alone on the bench, watching the others.)*

MATTHEW. The theme for this year's Senior Prom is A Night in Nineveh.

SIMON. Who says?

MATTHEW. I did. Peggy Powell, you're in charge of decorations.

BARTHOLOMEW/PEGGY. I need volunteers.

PETER. Me!

SIMON. Me!

JOHN. Me, Peggy!

PEGGY. I want Joshua.

JOSHUA. Sure, Peggy. Excuse Me, Mrs. McElroy.

MRS. McELROY. *(After him.)* Sonnet LXIV next time, my favorite. "The expense of spirit."

JOSHUA. *(Going.)* "In a waste of shame." I already know it. *(He has joined Peggy.)*

26

PEGGY. Are You in love with Mrs. McElroy?

JOSHUA. Don't be ridiculous, Peggy. She's an old woman. She's like 30 and she has two children.

PEGGY. You act like You're in love with her.

JOSHUA. Gross Me out, why don't you! She understands Me. My parents don't. Sometimes I don't think they're really My parents.

PEGGY. Every teenager feels like that. So who are You going to ask to the prom?

JOSHUA. I don't know. Who are you going with?

PEGGY. Dub Taylor and Spider Sloan and Billy Brown all asked me but I sort of told them all no. I sort of told them I was hoping someone else would ask me and if he didn't then maybe I'd go with Billy Brown but I would never go with Dub or Spider.

JAMES THE LESS/BILLY BROWN. He stares at me all the time.

JOHN/DUB TAYLOR. You mean in the shower.

BILLY BROWN. I don't just mean in the shower. I mean in home room, I mean in chemistry, I mean in civics.

PETER/SPIDER SLOAN. He's in love with you, Billy.

BILLY. BROWN Shut up, Spider.

DUB TAYLOR. Okay, so you're in love with Him.

BILLY BROWN. You, too, Dub. *(Peter, Simon and Matthew snap towels at each other, wrestle, etc.)*

PEGGY. They're coarse, uncouth rednecks. Billy's a little better but not much. So who do You want to ask as opposed to probably will because You think You should who or just because You're pretty sure she'll say yes who?

JOSHUA. Patricia Rudd.

THOMAS/PATRICIA. I'd love to, Joshua.

PEGGY. She's practically the ugliest girl in the whole school.

PATRICIA. Nuts to you, Peggy! Have another abortion nobody's supposed to know about!

ANDREW/BERT MOODY. Welcome to Pontius Pilate High Senior Class Prom. For those of you who have been living under a rock for the past four years, I am your on-his-way-to-med-school-like-a-rocket senior class president, Bert Moody. I want to thank Peggy and Joshua for the splendid decorations.

SIMON. Love that feminine touch, Joshua.

PATRICIA. Don't listen to them, Josh.

BERT MOODY. I have the winners of the Favorites Contest. Please step up to the bandstand as your name is called. Most Beautiful and Most Handsome. *(He opens an envelope.)*

PATRICIA. *(So what else is new?)* Peggy Powell and Beau Hunter.

BERT MOODY. For the fourth year in a row, the winners are Peggy Powell and Beau Hunter.

BEAU. I just want to say: blinding good looks aren't everything.

BERT MOODY. Very funny, Beau, very funny. We understand you'll be majoring in stand-up comedy at Texas Tech.

PEGGY. I believe Beau is speaking about inner beauty.

SIMON. He has to. Did you ever see the size of his dick!

MRS. McELROY. *(Ready to report names.)* Who said that? Who said that?

BERT MOODY. Most popular. Darlene Taylor and Bert Moody. Bert Moody, oh my God, that's me! Why thank you. Where's Darlene?

PETER. She's having her period.

MRS. McELROY. Who is saying these things? They are headed straight to Mr. Franklin's office.

PETER. Fuck Mr. Franklin.

BERT MOODY. Most Likely to Take It Up the Hershey Highway. Joshua. I don't know how this got in here. That wasn't funny. I'm sorry, Joshua. Most Likely To Succeed. Mary Swanson and Stanford Walsh. *(The band strikes up "Unchained Melody".* Simon sings while all the others Actors dance. Patricia and Joshua dance together D.)*

PATRICIA. What they did was stupid and cruel and why I am going to write the President of the United States telling him that if there is any place in this country where nuclear bomb testing should be allowed it's Corpus Christi, Texas. Ow!

JOSHUA. I'm sorry.

THADDEUS. May I cut in?

PATRICIA. I don't know.

JOSHUA. That's okay. *(He leaves them to dance together.)*

THADDEUS. Oh, God.

---

*See Special Note on Songs and Recordings on copyright page.

PATRICIA. What's wrong?

THADDEUS. I'm getting a hard on. *(He whirls her into the swirl of the other dancers. Everyone is dancing now but Joshua and Judas. Joshua moves away from them and takes out a pack of Lucky Strikes and lights one. He is outside the gym where the dance is being held now. Simon sings a song of the period.)*

GOD. This is my beloved Son in whom I take great delight.

JOSHUA. Who said that? Why won't You leave Me alone? *(Simon continues singing his song. James The Less, John and Peter appear. They will take a leak, smoke, check their hair, etc.)*

DUB TAYLOR. If you can't fuck her tonight, you're never gonna fuck her.

SPIDER SLOAN. Look who's talking!

BILLY BROWN. You'd be the only guy in Pontius Pilate High who hasn't fucked her. *(He sees Joshua.)* Well almost the only guy in Pontius Pilate High who hasn't fucked her. You haven't fucked Penny Porter have You, Joshua?

SPIDER SLOAN. Ssshhh! Can't you see He's trying to take a leak. The man can't take a leak with you yakking at him. *(Standing next to Joshua, shoulder-to-shoulder.)* Can He?

BILLY BROWN. That's the God's honest truth. *(On the other side of Joshua now.)* But you know what's worse than a guy yakking at you while you're trying to piss? It's a guy looking at your dick while you're trying to piss. I hate it when a guy does that. I hate it a lot.

DUB TAYLOR. What do you do to someone like that, Billy?

BILLY BROWN. Well the last guy who did that to me I beat the shit out of him and then I stuck his head in the toilet until he said he wasn't gonna look at anybody's dick while they were trying to take a piss ever again in his whole fucked-up fairy queer life.

DUB TAYLOR. I guess that was telling him.

BILLY. I guess it was. What do You say to that, Joshua?

SPIDER SLOAN. He can't say anything, Billy.

BILLY BROWN. Why not?

SPIDER SLOAN. He's too busy looking at your dick. *(Billy Brown and Dub Taylor try to duck Joshua's head in the urinal, yelling "Flush it, flush it.")*

JUDAS. Leave Him alone.

BILLY BROWN. We were just fooling around.

DUB TAYLOR. We didn't mean anything. Honest.

SPIDER SLOAN. Tell him. We were just. Okay, okay. We're gone. *(They are gone.)*

JOSHUA. Thank you.

JUDAS. Thank you? I save Your life and that's all I get? Thank you?

JOSHUA. I don't think they were actually going to kill Me.

JUDAS. You would have wished they had. I'm Judas.

JOSHUA. I'm Joshua.

JUDAS. I know. I've seen You. You don't have many friends. That's okay, I'll be Your friend. You talk to Yourself. "This is my Son in whom I take much delight." I've heard You. You can talk to me now.

JOSHUA. That wasn't Me.

JUDAS. Nobody here but us chickens. It must have been somebody.

JOSHUA. What are you staring at?

JUDAS. You. Does it bother You?

JOSHUA. No. I can stare right back.

JUDAS. First one who looks away has to buy a six-pack, okay?

JOSHUA. Okay. I always win this game.

JUDAS. So do I.

JOSHUA. Are we playing?

JUDAS. We're playing.

JOSHUA. Who'd you come with?

JUDAS. No one.

JOSHUA. How come?

JUDAS. I don't like girls. What about You?

JOSHUA. What do you mean, what about Me?

JUDAS. You like girls?

JOSHUA. Yes, I like girls.

JUDAS. Just asking, Joshua.

JOSHUA. I like boys, too. I like people.

JUDAS. You're lucky. I don't.

JOSHUA. Don't what?

JUDAS. Like people. You ever play the other side of "Heartbreak Hotel?" (*Joshua shakes his head.*) You never turned it over? (*Joshua shakes his head.*) That's the difference between us. Curiosity.

JOSHUA. I'm curious.

JUDAS. So who's Your favorite movie star?

JOSHUA. Marilyn Monroe.

JUDAS. She can't act.

JOSHUA. I don't care. I like her. She's pretty. What about James Dean?

JUDAS. He can't act either. I'd like to do it with him though.

JOSHUA. I beg your pardon?

JUDAS. I'd like to do it with him. You looked away. I win. What's my prize?

JOSHUA. You said a six-pack.

JUDAS. I got a better idea. (*He kisses Joshua on the lips. Patricia enters.*)

PATRICIA. There You are. I looked.

JUDAS. Hello.

JOSHUA. This is Judas. This is Patricia.

PATRICIA. I'll be on the dance floor. (*Patricia goes.*)

JOSHUA. We shouldn't have done that.

JUDAS. Who says? Open Your mouth next time somebody kisses You.

BERT MOODY. Last dance! Find the girl you came with for the absolutely last dance!

JOSHUA. I better get back.

JUDAS. See you. (*Joshua moves away and begins to dance with Patricia. The last dance is a very romantic arrangement. Judas disappears in the shadows.*)

BERT MOODY. As we bid a fond farewell to our four years at Pontius Pilate High, let us remember to drive safely home, forsaking all opportunities to imbibe the grape and respecting the virtue of the virgins we walked in here with. The Roman Prefect has asked me to remind you that the city gates will be locked at 1 A.M. and not reopen until 5 A.M. You are warned. *Quo vadis, amigo?* (*Music swells as Actors disperse. Joshua and Patricia are making* *out in a parked car. The music coming from the radio is a quiet version of "Amazing Grace."* We are aware of the glow of Judas' cigarette in the shadows.)*

JOSHUA. I love you, Patricia.

PATRICIA. Those aren't my tits, Josh. These are my tits. Are You sure You've done this before?

JOSHUA. Lots of times.

PATRICIA. Ouch!

JOSHUA. Sorry.

PATRICIA. We don't have to do this.

JOSHUA. But I want to.

PATRICIA. I don't think Your heart is really in it. I saw what You were doing with that guy, Josh. It's okay. I understand. I mean, I'm not going to throw up or anything.

JOSHUA. Would you like Me to take you home?

PATRICIA. The one night of your life you're supposed to stay out all night and come home at dawn with sand in your hair and try to convince your parents "of course I didn't go all the way" when of course that's exactly what you *did* do! Mine will never believe I'm still a virgin and it'll be true. This is what Mrs. McElroy means by dramatic irony.

JOSHUA. I'm sorry.

PATRICIA. You gotta stop saying that, Josh. It's getting to be a habit of Yours. I'm not going to let You humiliate me by taking me home now. We'll watch the sunrise. If You tell me Your biggest, deepest secret — the one You'd die if anyone else knew — maybe I'll tell You mine. *(They get out of the car. In the starry night we can see other couples lying on blankets on the beach. It is as if the whole world is making love.)* So? I'm listening.

JOSHUA. I hear hammering.

PATRICIA. When? Right now? That's the surf.

JOSHUA. All My life I've heard hammering. Like someone is building something and they never stop. Something for Me. And they're waiting for Me to what? I don't know.

PATRICIA. If that's Your biggest secret, no wonder You're weird. Mine is I'm in love with Spider Sloan even though I also hate him. It's called ambivalence.

---

*See Special Note on Songs and Recordings on copyright page.

JOSHUA. And sometimes I hear this voice. I never know when. It always says the same thing:

JUDAS. *(From the shadows.)* This is my Son in whom I take much delight.

PATRICIA. Who said that?

JUDAS. Hello, Patricia. Spider's right over there, he's nailing Laurie Paulson.

PATRICIA. I hate you. I hate you both. *(Patricia runs back to the bench.)*

JUDAS. *(After her.)* It's not my fault he thinks you're the ugliest girl in town.

JOSHUA. That was cruel.

JUDAS. She'll get over it. Besides, maybe it's my nature.

JOSHUA. I don't believe that. That's no one's nature.

JUDAS. What's Your nature, Joshua?

JOSHUA. I don't know. Kindness, I hope. Love. Respect for others.

JUDAS. I believe You. *(Judas pulls Joshua towards him.)*

JOSHUA. You can come no closer to Me than My body. Everything else you will never touch. Everything important is hidden from you.

JUDAS. Whatever. *(He kisses him. This time Joshua responds.)*

PATRICIA. All my life I will remember that night and every time I do, I will be so sad and angry it turned out the way it did. I know that's selfish. I mean, he was Joshua, after all, but we didn't know that then and I was just Patricia Rudd at the time but I wanted someone to love me so badly that night. Put that down, Tiffany! How many times do I have to tell you, young lady! When your father gets home! Excuse me. Goddamnit, Tiffany!

SPIDER SLOAN. About five and half years after that night (and yes, I plowed Laurie Paulson who later married my best friend, Billy Brown, I'm godfather to their three kids) I was in the service, really drunk one night, and I let this queer blow me. He was down there doing it and I said "Do you know Joshua?" and he shook his head no. I thought they all knew one another. I said "From up here you look like Joshua." I don't know what that makes me — it was one blow job for Christ's sake — but it doesn't make me one of them. Not a cocksucker but a cocksuck-ee, I guess. Nancy, where'd you hide my blue socks?

PEGGY.   What can I tell you? I certainly didn't know He was the Son of God, if that's what you're asking. You don't decorate your high school gym for your senior prom or edit the yearbook with someone you think is the Messiah. He wasn't boyfriend material, that's for certain.

MRS. McELROY.   I loved all my students. I can't pretend I had a favorite. I just wanted each of them to be true to himself (or herself) and reach his (or her) potential as a creative human being.

DUB TAYLOR.   He was. What? I can't put it in words. I would come to weep many tears for how we treated Him.

MRS. McELROY.   I was a high school English teacher. He was my student. One of many, many hundreds. I know how you would have liked me to say something else. I'm sorry. *(All the Actors save Joshua and Judas have returned to their places on the benches. Joshua and Judas are now young men.)*

JUDAS.   Had Judas lived a long life, he would have forgotten that night — and the many other nights.

JOSHUA.   Liquid Gulf Coast nights.

JUDAS.   He and Joshua shared. Nights he wished.

JOSHUA.   We both wished.

JUDAS.   Would never end.

JOSHUA.   Maybe he would have forgotten the night we painted "J & J 4VR" on the water tower and the next day nobody knew who J and J were but us.

JUDAS.   But because he did not grow old, all he remembered was what he could not have, he longed for what he could not have, and he grew twisted and envious and afraid. But not yet. That is later in our story.

JOHN.   Now began Joshua's many years of wandering. Years lost to us. He left no note. One morning, just like that, He was gone. Some say He went to China; others, India. I don't have to tell you where the Irish think He went. I personally don't think He ever left the state of Texas. *(Joshua picks up his things and begins to hitchhike. The roar of big trucks passing him by at high speeds is deafening.)*

TRUCK DRIVER. *(Whizzing by.)* Get a haircut!

JOSHUA. *(After him.)* Screw you!

2ND TRUCK DRIVER. Hot enough for You, shithead?

JOSHUA. I love you, too!

GOD. Joshua, the time has come to leave Corpus Christi and begin Your life as the son of Man.

JOSHUA. What does it look like I'm doing? I'm way ahead of You.

GOD. I'm sending You a messenger.

3RD TRUCK DRIVER. Hello, sonny, going my way?

JOSHUA. I am now.

3RD TRUCK DRIVER. Hop in.

JOSHUA. Thanks. What's that smell?

3RD TRUCK DRIVER. Just a little patch of leprosy on my right arm here. Guess it's time to change the ol' air-freshener. Tell me something: Am I on the right side of the road?

JOSHUA. What's the matter? You blind?

3RD TRUCK DRIVER. Not to worry, son. Blind since birth and behind the wheel since twelve. All's I need's my bearing and away we go. Hang on! *(He puts the truck in gear and it roars off.)* So where You headed?

JOSHUA. Anywhere you take Me.

3RD TRUCK DRIVER. Running away or running to?

JOSHUA. Just running. *(It quickly becomes night. The stars are blinding, the sky is midnight blue.)* It got so cold all of a sudden! *(He shivers.)*

3RD TRUCK DRIVER. That's the desert for you. This is the scary part of the trip. Miles and miles of desert up ahead. Nothing but sand and heat. Not a place you want to break down. I did once. Left me a changed man. I had to hug myself at night to stay warm and make my own shade at high noon. You ever been alone like that? It can drive a person crazy. I thought I saw Anita Ekberg offering me a glass of ice cold milk. She was a Swedish actress before Your time. Famous for her tits. I told her I loved her and she just laughed, the way all mirages mock and deceive us, and let the cold milk run down her creamy breasts

35

and vanished, only to appear again on the next horizon. We all have mirages we chase after. Mine was flesh. Wonder what Yours'll be?

JOSHUA.   Why are you telling Me all this?

3ʳᴰ TRUCK DRIVER.   Turn on the radio if You don't want Me talking Your ear off. 'Course all You're gonna get this time of night is religious fanatics. *(Joshua turns on the car radio.)*

GOD'S VOICE.   This is My Son in Whom I am well pleased.

3ʳᴰ TRUCK DRIVER.   What did I tell You? Sounds like He's trying to tell You something. *(Joshua turns off the radio.)* That ain't gonna make His voice go away.

JOSHUA.   All my life I've heard it. I don't know what it means.

3ʳᴰ TRUCK DRIVER.   He's saying He's well pleased with You.

JOSHUA.   How can He be pleased with Me when I am so displeased with Myself?

3ʳᴰ TRUCK DRIVER.   He has given You the gift of healing. Touch me.

JOSHUA.   I don't want to touch you.

3ʳᴰ TRUCK DRIVER.   Touch me! *(He takes Joshua's hands and puts them on his eyes.)* Thank You, Lord! I can see. My skin is smooth. The air is sweet. I am healed of all affliction. He has given you the greatest gift of all, Son of God.

JOSHUA.   Don't call Me that! I'm not worthy.

3ʳᴰ TRUCK DRIVER.   Then become worthy. Now get out. The world is waiting for You. Get out, I said! *(Joshua gets out.)*

JOSHUA.   Who are you? Tell me.

3ʳᴰ TRUCK DRIVER.   Ask a *hard* question next time. *Hasta luego, amigo! (He is gone.)*

JOSHUA.   Wait! Don't leave Me here! I'll die out here. Is that what you want? *(All the Actors start to leave the stage.)* Where are you going? Wait. Come back! Don't leave me. *(All the other Actors have gone. Joshua is utterly alone in a pool of light that becomes the terrible burning desert.)* I'll wait. Someone else will come. *(Pause. In the distance, we hear what sounds like a truck approaching.)* Here comes someone. Stop! Slow down! *(The sounds of a large truck barreling by him on the highway. The force of it sends Joshua flying.)* A mirage. The old man was right. *(James [Jimmy] Dean appears. He wears a red windbreaker.)*

JIMMY. You okay? *(He helps Joshua up.)*

JOSHUA. Jimmy?

JIMMY. Where You headed?

JOSHUA. I don't know.

JIMMY. Anyplace is better than here. Somebody told me You saw *East of Eden* 12 times?

JOSHUA. And *Rebel Without a Cause* ten.

JIMMY. What about *Giant*?

JOSHUA. Just once.

JIMMY. What's wrong with *Giant*?

JOSHUA. Nothing. It wasn't about Me.

JIMMY. That's selfish.

JOSHUA. I know.

JIMMY. Not everything can be about You, Joshua.

JOSHUA. Well, also you got old in it and died at the end.

JIMMY. I didn't die. I was just dead drunk. *(He points.)* That's how I died. That Porsche with the buzzards sitting on it. You know how You're going to die?

JOSHUA. No.

JIMMY. You want to know?

JOSHUA. No.

JIMMY. What's wrong?

JOSHUA. And God so loved the world He gave His only Son to it.

JIMMY. And He chose You?

JOSHUA. I don't want to be different, Jimmy. I want to be like everyone else. I want to be happy.

JIMMY. Sure You do.

JOSHUA. I want to love someone.

JIMMY. I know, I know.

JOSHUA. I want someone to love Me. I want My life to matter.

JIMMY. Come here. *(Judas appears from U. and joins Joshua.)* Don't worry. I've got You. It's a long way down. Now what do You see down there, shimmering in the sun?

JOSHUA. A great city.

JIMMY. Welcome to Your new kingdom, Your Majesty. How do You like it?

JOSHUA. It's amazing.

JIMMY. Just say the word and it's Yours.

JOSHUA. What do I have to do?

JIMMY. Almost nothing.

JOSHUA. Tell me. What?

JIMMY. It's so little it's hardly worth mentioning .

JOSHUA. What?

JIMMY. A moment later and You won't even remember You've done it.

JOSHUA. What?

JIMMY. Deny You're the Son of God.

JOSHUA. But I am the Son of God.

JIMMY. Deny it anyway. I did and look at me, King of the World! You will feel nothing but Yourself. Your needs, Your pleasures. It's a small price for all that. Are You ready?

JOSHUA. It would be a lie.

JIMMY. Think long and hard, Joshua. I offer You all the pleasures of His earthly kingdom. He offers You a wooden cross. (*A Crucified Man appears in Joshua's delirium.*) See Yourself, Joshua. That is His promise. Down there is mine. Choose.

JOSHUA. I have chosen. I want to see God. I want to know Him. You are no friend of Mine. Get thee behind Me. (*Judas flings Joshua off the precipice.*)

JUDAS. Satan cursed Him and was gone. He would seek Judas to do his work.

PETER. Joshua had endured His time in the desert. He had embraced His destiny. His time had come. He would live as the Son of God in peace and love with all men. He had found His way to the city and — I'm happy to say:

ALL. Us! (*All the Actors become this great city. Lots of noise and activity.*)

PETER. Fish! Get your fresh fish here. I have eels. I have snapper! I have lung! I've got perch. I've got scrod. I've got rhythm. (*Joshua approaches, weak from hunger.*) I've got a customer. Hi.

JOSHUA. They look good.

PETER. They are good. I caught them myself. What can I get You?

JOSHUA.   I don't have any money.

PETER.   You and everybody else. How do You expect to live?

JOSHUA.   I don't know. The kindness of strangers?

PETER.   I wouldn't count on it.

JOSHUA.   The Bible says the Lord will provide.

PETER.   I'm not the Lord. Nothing's for free. *(He resumes hawking.)* I have squid! I have sole! *(He stops.)* Are You just going to stand there like that?

JOSHUA.   It's a free country.

PETER.   Until some Roman centurion cracks Your skull open because he doesn't like the way You looked at him. When was the last time You ate?

JOSHUA.   I don't remember.

PETER.   All right, I'll give You one. They're just going to spoil anyway.

JOSHUA.   Are you always this generous?

PETER.   Almost never. Don't tell anyone. I don't want to get a reputation. *(Peter puts one fresh fish in a basket and hands it to Joshua.)*

JOSHUA.   Thank you. What's your name?

PETER.   Peter. Simon Peter. *(A Poor Woman approaches.)*

JAMES THE LESS/POOR WOMAN.   Please, sir? It's not for me. My children are starving.

PETER.   See what You started?

POOR WOMAN.   We'll take anything.

PETER.   What do you think I'm running? I'm a fishmonger, not a charity. Go to the poorhouse. They'll feed you.

JOSHUA.   Here, take Mine. *(He gives her his fish.)*

POOR WOMAN.   Thank You, young man.

PETER.   What are You doing? She's a beggar.

JOSHUA.   So am I.

PETER.   She's not one of us.

JOSHUA.   She is all of us. You say you have children?

POOR WOMAN.   Five.

JOSHUA.   What are their names?

POOR WOMAN.   Antony, Julia, Mark, Flor and Joseph, he's the littlest. *(Joshua will take five fish from the basket Peter gave him.)*

JOSHUA. This is for Antony, this is for Julia, one for Mark, here's Flor's and this one is for little Joseph. My father is called Joseph.

POOR WOMAN. God Bless You! *(She spontaneously throws her arms around him. She exits.)*

PETER. I gave You one fish. You gave her five.

JOSHUA. You would have given her none.

PETER. It was a miracle.

JOSHUA. I asked and they were given. You could have given her five hundred fish. You said so yourself: they'll only spoil. Who were you saving them for? You have a big heart. Simon Peter. You opened it to Me. Open it to everyone. There's room in there for all of us. Listen with this ... *(He puts his hand on Peter's heart.)* — not with what others have told you you must do. When we don't love one another, we don't love God. *(Peter puts his hand on Joshua's heart.)* Do you hear Him?

PETER. I hear Your heart beating.

JOSHUA. Then you hear God.

PETER. I'm trembling.

JOSHUA. Me, too. You are My brother. If you are wretched, I am wretched, too. *(They embrace)*

PETER. *(To us.)* Was it really like this, are you wondering? Yes, it was. I think it always is when Joshua or Jesus or whatever you want to call Him is revealed to you. The false images fall away. In your heart there is a sudden burning sensation, a fire.

JOSHUA. We will go where God the Father takes us. We will teach His word. Make it new again. Will you come with Me?

JOHN. And Peter put down his nets and went with Him. There were a lot of free fish that day! Soon, very soon, in fact, there were five of us. I remember I was in a park. This young guy was speaking. He had a nice little crowd. I started writing down what He said.

JOSHUA. Love the Lord God your Father by loving one another. That is where He is, in each of us, not in temples or false idols. *(To John.)* You don't have to write down what I say. You're not in school. Do it! Open your hearts to each other. I was alone for so long. Now I have a brother in this man. *(He puts his arm around Peter.)* But I'm greedy. I want more.

PETER. We adored Him. We would have followed Him to the ends of the earth. He was our leader.

JOSHUA. *(Protesting.)* God is our leader. I'm just this guy like you. No better, no worse. I can't gut a fish, Peter, and I don't think I ever want to. I couldn't begin to cut someone's hair, Thaddeus. God knows, I can't sing. You've all heard Me. But when you do, Simon, you're singing for Me, saying things I can't. John writes down everything I say, which is good, because I don't remember half the time. We're each special. We're each ordinary. We're each divine.

THOMAS. What about me? You left me out.

JOSHUA. I'm sorry. You're very special, Thomas.

THOMAS. Thank you.

JOSHUA. You're very ordinary.

THOMAS. Thank you.

JOSHUA. And you're very divine. *(Andrew erupts from his place on the bench.)*

ANDREW. Fuck you, fuck you. Help me. Eat shit. Die. Help me. Fuck you, fuck you. Help me!

PETER. Be careful! He's possessed by a demon. Get away from us!

ANDREW. Help me, please. Heal me.

JOSHUA. Let Me hold you, brother.

ANDREW. Sir, if only (fuck you, fuck you) You will (fuck your mother, fuck your father), You can drive the evil spirit out (fuck God!) and make me clean again.

JOSHUA. I will try. *(Joshua holds Andrew fiercely to him.)* Father, if it is Thy will, let Me drive the demon from this man. Satan, be gone.

JUDAS. And he was.

PETER. Look, there he goes!

JOSHUA. Be clean again, as you were as a child.

ANDREW. It's stopped. It's a miracle. *(Bartholomew and James leap from their place on the bench.)*

BARTHOLOMEW. That wasn't medicine. That was witchcraft.

JOSHUA. Why are you so angry, brother?

BARTHOLOMEW. I'm not Your brother. I'm a doctor. Two hours ago, a young man died in my arms at the hospital. His skin

41

was yellow. He weighed 93 pounds. He was going to be a doctor. "Help me," he said. His eyes were still bright. They looked right at me. "Help me." I couldn't save him with all my skills and medicines and love and neither could You. We don't need Messiahs. We need cures.

JOSHUA. I have no answer for you.

BARTHOLOMEW. Then why should I follow You?

JOSHUA. You are a man who has lost faith.

BARTHOLOMEW. What planet have You been living on? We've all lost faith.

JAMES. He didn't mean that.

BARTHOLOMEW. Don't tell me what I mean James. I'm not one of your students. *(He goes back to the bench and sits.)*

JAMES. I'm sorry. He hasn't slept in three days. He's a good man.

JOSHUA. I believe that, James. *(James joins Bartholomew.)* Well, so be it. We've got a lot of work to do.

SIMON. But it never felt like work.

THOMAS. We did what are called good deeds. With Joshua it seemed impossible there could be any other kind.

JOHN. Of course we got into trouble, too. People were listening to Him and there were more and more of us. The authorities didn't like that.

JAMES THE LESS. Finally someone was telling the truth. We weren't free. We were slaves of Rome. My first night with Him and we all ended up in jail.

MATTHEW. That's when you all decided you needed a good lawyer.

JOSHUA. No, that's when you decided we needed a good lawyer, Matthew.

THADDEUS. And then there were the Saturday nights. We had some pretty wonderful Saturday nights. *(The other disciples have brought forward a bright and gaudy Wurlitzer juke box. Everyone starts dancing. All the disciples are present — even the ones who haven't "met" Joshua yet. They dance alone and/or in appropriate combinations: James The Less and Matthew, Bartholomew and James. High above them all is a go-go boy. It is Philip. He has bells on his feet.)*

JUDAS. Want to dance?

JOSHUA. Judas!

JUDAS. I thought it was You. How long has it been? Let me get a look at You. You're a man now.

JOSHUA. We both are.

JUDAS. The boy has become a master.

JOSHUA. Are you rich?

JUDAS. Can't You tell?

JOSHUA. Are you powerful?

JUDAS. Beyond my wildest dreams. I own three restaurants. Just try to get a reservation. What about You?

JOSHUA. I'm happy.

JUDAS. I believe You. Your eyes are shining.

JOSHUA. So are yours.

JUDAS. I'm happy to see You. *(He takes a hit on a popper.)* I'm on my way to oblivion. Care to join me?

JOSHUA. You don't need that.

JUDAS. You're right; I don't. *(He takes another hit. Philip approaches.)*

JOSHUA. Who's that?

THOMAS. Ignore him, Josh. He's bad news.

JAMES. He's not interested, Philip.

PHILIP. You're all interested. I have bells on my ankles. Hear them? Tinkle, tinkle, tinkle. I'm ringing them just for You, Joshua. Tinkle, tinkle, tinkle.

PETER. Ignore him, Josh.

PHILIP. Can't You speak for Yourself, master? Don't You want a little slave boy tonight?

JOSHUA. They told Me you were a hustler.

PHILIP. I am. They all want me, that's why they hate me. I know who likes it rough, who likes it sweet, who likes it fast, who likes it slow. I bet You I know how You like it, Joshua.

PETER. Get away from us you little disease-ridden, filthy whore! You're talking to the Son of God.

JOSHUA. And He is listening. Why are you so quick to judge others? All of you.

PHILIP. It's all right. I don't hear them anymore. You want me, don't You, Joshua?

JOSHUA. I don't have any money.

PHILIP. What can You pay me with?

JOSHUA. My life. I have nothing else to give you.

PHILIP. I could take that from You. It wouldn't be the first time.

OTHERS. Don't go with him! He's dangerous! He's sick! *(Joshua and Philip disappear through the others. The disco music stops.)*

PHILIP. Get undressed. You got five minutes. Did You hear what I said?

JOSHUA. I love you.

PHILIP. Say what?

JOSHUA. I love you, Philip.

PHILIP. I love You, too, Charlie. I hope You have rubbers. I'm positive.

JOSHUA. I said I love you.

PHILIP. Hey! Don't fuck with me. You love the idea of telling someone like me You love them. It makes You feel good. Love this.

JOSHUA. I think I can heal you. I think I can make you well.

PHILIP. I think You can suck my dick now, faggot. *(Joshua goes to Philip and takes him by both arms and looks directly into his eyes.)*

JOSHUA. Father, heal this man.

PHILIP. Fuck You.

JOSHUA. Let these hands make him well. Give him back his life.

PHILIP. Fuck You, I said.

JOSHUA. You are healed, Philip.

PHILIP. I wish I could believe that.

JOSHUA. Then do. As you believe, so shall you be. You are healed, I say. *(Philip kneels before Joshua, his head is bowed.)*

PHILIP. I was going to beat the shit out of You and take Your wallet.

JOSHUA. There wasn't anything in it.

PHILIP. I am not worthy to kiss Your feet.

PETER. None of us are.

PHILIP. And from the moment these lips kissed His feet, Philip was happy. It didn't matter who he'd been. He was well again, body and soul.

PETER. I'm sorry, Philip, I wronged you. We all did. *(One by one all the Actors will cross to Joshua and kiss his feet. Simon will sing a hymn in his beautiful clear light tenor until it is his turn. Bartholomew, James and Matthew stand apart from the others now.)*

JOSHUA. Do you believe, Bartholomew, I have the power to do what you want but cannot? As you believe, let it be.

BARTHOLOMEW. Is it possible?

JOSHUA. You saw with your own eyes.

JAMES. We did, Bart, we saw.

BARTHOLOMEW. Let me heal my brothers. That is all I ask. *(Bartholomew prostrates himself before Joshua and kisses his feet.)*

PETER. Are you with us?

JUDAS. Sure, why not? *(He kisses Joshua's feet. Now only Matthew stands apart.)*

MATTHEW. I'm sorry, gentlemen, but I have a lot of trouble kissing someone's feet.

JAMES THE LESS. Joshua isn't someone.

MATTHEW. I think it's degrading. It reeks of servitude. It's the language of slaves.

JAMES THE LESS. That's not what it's saying. *(Joshua has come to where Matthew is standing.)*

JOSHUA. I love you, Matthew.

MATTHEW. You're not better than me, Joshua. I can't accept that.

JOSHUA. I am less than you. *(Joshua prostrates himself and kisses Matthew's feet. Matthew puts his face in his hands and weeps.)*

JOHN. Matthew never went back to his office at the law firm. Instead, he gave away everything he owned. His home. His car. His father's ring. Everything.

PETER. We were 12. *(The disciples come together, happily embracing each other. Music. Laughter.)*

JOHN. The days that followed were glorious. We lived hand to mouth but we didn't care. We never went hungry. Someone always fed us.

THOMAS. I loved the miracles, even if I didn't get one of my own. Walk! See! Hear! I couldn't do them, of course, none of us could, but I loved watching Joshua.

BARTHOLOMEW. We slept in fields. I saw my first eclipse. I helped a woman give birth: amazing.

PETER. All 13 of us, arm in arm, we were quite a sight. We were so fucking cool it hurt.

JOSHUA. *(An admonishment.)* Peter.

PETER. Right. (But we were!)

SIMON. There was an old man named Lazarus. He'd been dead for six days and was starting to smell to high heaven. He had a wife and six daughters. I wish you could have heard the racket they were making. *(And we do as the disciples become the wailing women. They are loud. Thomas is Lazarus.)*

JOSHUA. Arise, Lazarus.

SIMON. I think this was one of the practical miracles. I mean, there was no big reason for it. Lazarus wasn't a big cheese or even an especially nice guy. Joshua just couldn't stand the noise. *(Increased wailing from the women.)*

JOSHUA. Shut up women. Thank you. I say Lazarus, arise. *(Lazarus suddenly sits up.)*

LAZARUS. *(To the women.)* What is the matter with you? You'd think you'd seen a ghost!

JOSHUA. You have been asleep, Lazarus — not for six days but for all the years of your life. Now live as if your very life depended on it.

LAZARUS. How do I live? Teach me.

JOSHUA. Be awake every moment and give thanks to God the Father for it. Give back as much, no, more! than you have been given. Laugh. Fill your lungs with His good air and pray. You have all forgotten to pray.

LAZARUS. *(Kneeling, head lowered.)* God, forgive this wretched sinner.

JOSHUA. Not like that: on your knees, head bowed, your eyes closed! You're not afraid of Him. Like this: standing tall, eyes open, smiling even, your arms open to His love. This is how we talk to God. Our Father which art in heaven, Hallowed be Thy name. Thy kingdom come. Thy will be done on earth, as it is in heaven. Give us this day our daily bread. And forgive us our debts as we forgive our debtors. And lead us not into temptation,

46

but deliver us from evil: For Thine is the kingdom and the power and the glory, for ever. Alleluia!

ALL. Alleluia!

JAMES THE LESS. Everywhere we went we found great crowds awaiting us at every bend in the road.

SIMON. People were desperate for some message. They had lost their way.

PHILIP. Young people flocked to Him. He understood them. They hung on His every word.

JOSHUA. Love thy neighbor as thyself.

THADDEUS/CENTURION. Sir, if I may.

BARTHOLOMEW. (*Sarcastically.*) A Roman centurion! Have you come to arrest us? Or just beat us up this time? Be careful, we have a very good lawyer now.

JOSHUA. Why are you such bastards? What little love you have. This man's eyes are red from weeping. Forgive my friends. Speak. You are welcome.

CENTURION. My wife is dying. You're our only hope.

JOSHUA. I will come.

PHILIP. Don't go. It's a trap.

JAMES THE LESS. He's one of the enemy.

JOSHUA. Such words make you Mine. James The Less was for your stature but it is also for your heart. Lead the way.

CENTURION. Sir, we are not worthy to have You in our home. You have only to say the word and she will be cured.

JOSHUA. Go home. Your wife is waiting for you. As you believe, so let it be. (*Centurion goes.*) Truly, I tell you, nowhere in Israel have I found such faith, not even among My own disciples.

JAMES THE LESS. What You teach comes easily from the lips, but so much harder from the heart. Help me.

JOSHUA. Love the Lord thy God with your heart and soul. Forgive your greatest enemy.

JAMES THE LESS. I can't.

JOSHUA. You must. I require mercy, not sacrifice. I do not say 70 times but seven times 70. Nothing more, nothing less.

JAMES THE LESS. I'm not ready.

JOSHUA. Would that we were all as honest as this man.

BARTHOLOMEW.   It was the same afternoon He preached the Sermon on the Mount. It seemed there was nothing He couldn't do. We were coming home from it, home that week being under an oak tree by a creek, when we encountered the same Centurion. *(The Centurion returns.)*

JOSHUA.   There's our friend. How is she?

CENTURION.   I was too late. She was dead.

JOSHUA.   I'm sorry.

PETER.   It was God's will, Josh. You said so Yourself.

JOSHUA.   Well, it wasn't mine! *(Then.)* I'm so ashamed. Forgive Me, all of you.

PETER.   And from that time there were fewer miracles of the flesh, but more and more miracles of the heart, simple acts that were worth three dozen exorcisms.

JAMES.   Bartholomew and I had wanted our union blessed for a long time — some acknowledgment of what we were to each other.

BARTHOLOMEW.   We asked, Josh. They said it was against the law and the priests said it was forbidden by scripture.

JAMES.   "If a man lies with a man as with a woman, both of them have committed an abomination; they shall be put to death, their blood is upon them."

JOSHUA.   Why would you memorize such a terrible passage? "And God saw everything that He had made, and behold it was very good." I can quote scripture as well as the next man. God loves us most when we love each other. We accept you and bless you. Who's got a ring?

JAMES.   Will You do it?

JOSHUA.   If you say nobody else will!

BARTHOLOMEW.   Out here? Someone might see.

JOSHUA.   Where would you be married, Bartholomew? Down a dark hole? We will marry you in broad daylight under the canopy of Heaven in the eyes of God and for all men to see. I said, who's got a ring?

PHILIP.   You can borrow mine. Okay, okay, *have!*

JOSHUA.   Who's got another one? Judas?

JUDAS.   Sorry, I can't.

THOMAS.   Take mine.

PETER. The priests will have something to say about this, Joshua.

JOSHUA. The priests have something to say about everything. Let's have some music. Who wants to give the groom away?

JOHN. I will!

JAMES. I'm the groom!

JOSHUA. Who wants to give the other groom away?

JAMES THE LESS. I'll do it. *(James and Bartholomew stand in front of Joshua.)*

JOSHUA. It is good when two men love as James and Bartholomew do and we recognize their union. No giggling back there! Now, take each other's hand. Love each other in sickness and health. Respect the divinity in your partner, Bartholomew. Cherish the little things in him, James, exalt in the great. May the first face you see each morning and the last at night always be his. I bless this marriage in Your name, Father. Amen. Now let's all get very, very drunk.

BARTHOLOMEW. You are truly the Messiah, Son of the living God. *(Matthew enters as the High Priest.)*

JOSHUA. Have you come to bless this marriage, too, father?

MATTHEW/HIGH PRIEST. It is one thing to preach Your perversions to ignorant and sentimental men and women such as yourselves but such travesties of God's natural order will never be blessed in the House of the Lord by one of His ordained priests.

JOSHUA. This is the House of the Lord. I ordain Myself.

HIGH PRIEST. You have broken every commandment.

JOSHUA. You are hypocrites. You are liars. You have perverted My Father's words to make them serve your ends. I despise you. *(Joshua sends the High Priest flying with a single blow.)*

THOMAS. Joshua, You struck a priest.

JOSHUA. And I'll do it again. All who do not love all men are against Me!

THOMAS. But You said we must always turn the other cheek.

JOSHUA. I must have been in a very good mood. Do not take everything I say so seriously. *(The high spirits of the wedding celebration have been quickly deflated.)*

PETER. Joshua.

JOSHUA. Not now, Peter.

PETER. Let me.

JOSHUA. I said not now. Go out and preach the Gospel. That is what disciples do.

JOHN. We don't know how.

JOSHUA. You don't know how to speak the truth?

THOMAS. They want to hear You.

JOSHUA. The Word is the Word, not the man who speaks it. What an unbelieving and perverse generation. What will you do when I am no longer with you?

JUDAS. I'll stay with Him. *(The other disciples disperse. Joshua puts his head in Judas' lap.)* That's better. *(He strokes Joshua's head.)*

JOSHUA. I get so angry.

JUDAS. I know. Ssshh. Sleep now. *(Sounds of crickets. Night. The campfire is very low. Simon stands looking down at Joshua sleeping in Judas' lap.)*

SIMON. One night we were around the fire. Just the two of us. He'd just performed the miracle of the loaves and fishes. Five loaves and two fish fed 5,000 men, not counting the women and children. Amazing! And 12 baskets were left over. I remember an owl hooting and thinking I'd never seen so many stars, so much stuff up there to wonder about. And for what seemed like an eternity, the two of us were one. Afterwards, He said the strangest thing.

JOSHUA. *(Murmuring in his sleep.)* You can come no closer to Me than your body, Simon. Everything else you will never touch. Everything important is hidden from you.

JUDAS. He said the same thing to me when we were boys together on a beach in Corpus Christi.

SIMON. What did He mean?

JUDAS. I don't know.

SIMON. Good night, Judas.

JUDAS. Good night, Simon. *(To us.)* What will you give me to betray Him to you? You know my price. Thirty pieces of silver. Not much for a place in history. Most of you will pass away quietly in your beds, or gasping for air in some miserable hospital and your goings will be as unremarkable as your lives. Think about it. *(High Priest tosses a bag of coins that land in front of Judas.)*

50

HIGH PRIEST. Thirty pieces of silver. You boys make it very easy for us.

JUDAS. Thank you, Father, we try.

HIGH PRIEST. But this one, He's a dangerous man.

JUDAS. What is His crime?

HIGH PRIEST. Blasphemy.

JUDAS. Because He says He's the Son of God?

HIGH PRIEST. No, because He says you're the Son of God as well.

JUDAS. We're all the Son of God.

HIGH PRIEST. Unless you're looking for trouble, I would keep that to myself. The Son of God is a cocksucker? I don't think so. We need sinners.

JUDAS. Last chance for immortality; going, going gone. Sold to the fag haters in priest's robes.

HIGH PRIEST. Good Passover, Judas Iscariot.

JUDAS. Happy Easter to you, rabbi. *(High Priest goes. Joshua wakes up in Judas' lap.)* Hello, sleepyhead.

JOSHUA. Where is everybody?

JUDAS. They're all sleeping. No one here but us chickens. You fell asleep in my lap, just like old times.

JOSHUA. I couldn't dance. Didn't know how to dress. No car. What did you ever see in Me?

JUDAS. Everything.

JOSHUA. Are you crying?

JUDAS. I never cry, You know that. When did You ever see me cry?

JOSHUA. Will you cry when they kill Me?

JUDAS. Nobody's going to kill You.

JOSHUA. Do you love Me?

JUDAS. Yes.

JOSHUA. Promise Me you'll be there when they do.

JUDAS. I promise.

JOSHUA. Then let's go home and end this.

JUDAS. Corpus Christi.

JOSHUA. Corpus Christi. *(A burst of joyful music. The other disciples get to their feet. They wave palms and sing. Some of them whirl like dervishes. Joshua rides on Thaddeus' back. A delirious pandemonium.)*

51

DISCIPLES. *(Variously.)* Hail, Joshua! Hail, the son of Man! Hail, the New Messiah!

SIMON. How does it feel to be home? You left in shame, return in triumph.

JOSHUA. Nothing's changed yet everything's different.

PEOPLE. Hail! Hail! Hail!

JOSHUA. Listen! *(Sudden, utter silence with the sweep of his hand.)* The hammering. It's stopped. Their work is done. The trap is set.

PHILIP/CARPENTER. In Your honor, for Passover, I have fashioned a table for You and Your disciples. That is the hammering You heard.

JOSHUA. My father was a carpenter. They tell Me he was a good one. *(The disciples will bring out a long table.)*

CARPENTER. A good carpenter is worth his weight in gold. A man who can do something with his hands. Anyone can preach about love. But it takes a man to build a good, solid table.

JOSHUA. We need a room to celebrate Passover.

PHILIP. It has been prepared for You, master. Everything is just as it should be.

JOHN. The supper. *(The stage picture should look like Da Vinci's.)*

THADDEUS. We were in that part of Corpus called Gethsemane. The meal that night was delicious. Peter and James outdid themselves on the lamb.

PETER. The secret is all in the marinade.

JAMES. And slow roasting. Slow, slow, slow.

THOMAS. Josh, there's a woman outside who says she is Your mother.

JOSHUA. Tell her I have no mother. You are My mother and father and brothers and sisters. You are My family now. We are all mother, father, brothers and sisters, each to the other. Now do you understand?

ANDREW. We looked at each other and we did.

PHILIP. It was breathtaking.

JAMES THE LESS. A perfect moment.

BARTHOLOMEW. A defining one.

THADDEUS. A moment later and He took away our breath again.

JOSHUA. One of you will betray Me this very night.

THOMAS. You're joking. He's joking!

PHILIP. He's not.

MATTHEW. Surely You don't mean one of us, Josh?

JOSHUA. One who has shared many meals with Me. One who has lain with Me. One who has said he loves Me and knows that I love him.

THOMAS. That could be any one of us. See? I told you He was joking.

JOSHUA. Alas for that man. It would be better for that man if he had never been born.

SIMON. Is it I, Lord?

JOHN. Is it I?

MATTHEW. Is it me, Josh?

THOMAS. Not I, Lord, surely?

JAMES THE LESS. It could never be me.

PETER. Not I, Josh.

JOSHUA. No, but before the cock crows you will betray Me three times this night, Peter.

PETER. I will cut off both my hands first.

BARTHOLOMEW. Is it one of us?

JAMES. You married us.

PHILIP. Me, Joshua?

THADDEUS. I know what you're all thinking — he's just a silly hairdresser — but it's not going to be me.

ANDREW. Is it I?

JUDAS. Is it I, Lord?

JOSHUA. Judas, you have said it. I have counted every hair on your head.

JUDAS. You're drunk, Josh. Who would betray the Son of God and be damned for all eternity? He's drunk, guys. It's the wine talking.

JOSHUA. When I am gone.

JUDAS. No one's going anywhere. Can we have some music, Simon? A little Bo Diddely. *(Simon obliges. A festive mood struggles to re-establish itself. Joshua speaks over it.)*

JOSHUA. I say when I am gone I will always be with you.

THOMAS. That doesn't even make sense, Josh. How can You be with us if You're gone?

JOSHUA. Take this bread and eat it in remembrance of Me. This bread is My body. Take this wine and drink. It is My blood. *(Hilarity from the others. Some of them start a bread fight. Others are gurgling wine.)*

THADDEUS. Yada-yada-yada!

PHILIP. Take this salt shaker. It is my life.

PETER. Eat this knife. It is my gall bladder.

ANDREW. I want to dance. Everybody dance. *(Some of the apostles already are.)*

SIMON. I'm crocked to the gills!

JAMES THE LESS. We all are, ain't it terrific?

THADDEUS. Happy Chanukah everyone!

THOMAS. It's Passover, you ape.

MATTHEW. Who's counting?

THADDEUS. Who are you calling an ape? *(All the apostles are clowning around, dancing, standing on the table, having a terrific time. Only Joshua and Judas remain still at the table. Joshua stands up.)*

JOSHUA. My appointed time is near. I am going out to the garden to pray. Will you wait up for Me?

ANDREW. If we don't run out of wine and music!

PHILIP. Sure we will, Josh.

JUDAS. I'll come with You. *(The other apostles recede U. as Joshua and Judas cross down to the Garden of Gethsemane.)* I'll be right over here. *(He sits apart from Joshua. Joshua prays.)*

JOSHUA. Father, I'm frightened. My hands are shaking. My stomach is so tight I can hardly breathe. I wipe My brow of sweat and it's blood. I'm angry, too! I don't want to die. Let this cup pass from Me. Don't make Me drink from it. I chose to be Your Son. I can *un*-choose. *(A burst of music and laughter from the apostles within.)* Why must I die for them? They don't deserve what You ask of Me. Will it hurt? I asked You a question: Will it hurt when the nails pierce the palms of My hands? *(Silence.)* Why don't You answer Me? *(Silence.)* Take Me to You soon. *(Joshua goes to where Judas has been waiting for him.)*

JUDAS. Did He tell You He loved You?

54

JOSHUA.   No. He didn't say anything. I'm ready. Are you? *(The other Actors are lying on the floor, as if passed out from too much food and wine.)* Couldn't you even wait up with Me one night? This night of all the others? *(Now there are three loud knocks on the door, as at the very beginning of the play. The disciples wake up in panic. They scatter and "hide"; i.e., they turn away from the playing area and become other characters again. Only Joshua and Judas remain.)*

JUDAS.   You brought this on Yourself, son of Man.

JOSHUA.   So did you, Judas.

ROMAN OFFICER.   Which one of you calls Himself the son of Man and the Messiah?

JUDAS.   I recognize You as Jesus of Galilee, known as Joshua of Corpus Christi, the son of Man and my true Redeemer. *(He kisses Joshua. Joshua kisses him back, hard.)*

ROMAN OFFICER.   Take Him. *(Joshua is seized and surrounded by the others. Peter is the only one of the apostles to step forward. To defend Joshua. His sword is drawn.)*

PETER.   Anyone who touches this man answers to Simon Peter.

THOMAS/SOLDIER.   I'm quaking in my boots! *(Peter strikes him with his sword.)* Ow!

PETER.   Who's next?

SOLDIER.   You cut off my ear.

PETER.   *(Ready for the next one.)* Come on, come on!

SOLDIER.   You cut off my fucking ear.

PETER.   I'll cut off your fucking balls!

JOSHUA.   Put up your sword, Peter. All who live by the sword shall die by the sword. Don't you think I could call a hundred angels to defend Me if I wanted? *(He goes to wounded Soldier.)* Here.

SOLDIER.   Get away from me! *(Joshua puts his hand on the Soldier's head and restores his ear.)*

JOSHUA.   God be with you, brother. *(To Soldiers.)* I'm ready.

JOHN.   The man was much amazed.

SOLDIER.   Holy shit!

JOHN.   As were we all. Before we knew it, they had taken Him. Except for Peter, we never saw Him again. We were cowards. We fled. How quickly it all ended.

JUDAS. What happens next is awful and beggars all description. I think we should stop here, gentlemen.

PHILIP. You began it, Judas, now tell it to the end. *(He thrusts a Bible at Judas who reads from it with growing difficulty and anguish.)*

JUDAS. "They bound Him and mocked Him. Then did they spit in His face and buffet Him. And others smote Him with the palms of their hands, saying:

BARTHOLOMEW. Prophesy unto us, Thou Christ, who is he that smote Thee? Smack!

THADDEUS. Was it me? Smack!

SIMON. Or was it me? Smack!

THADDEUS/BARTHOLOMEW/SIMON. Or maybe it was all three of us? Smack, smack, smack!!!

JUDAS. When the morning was come, all the chief priests took counsel against Him to put Him to death and they delivered Him to Pontius Pilate, the governor."

PHILIP/PILATE. What are the charges against Him?

ANDREW/PILATE'S WIFE. Have nothing to do with this man, husband. I had a dream of Him last night. He is innocent.

PILATE. Art Thou a queer then?

JOSHUA. Thou sayest I am.

PILATE. What do You say?

JOSHUA. To this end I was born and for this cause: I came into the world, that I should bear witness unto the truth.

PILATE. The truth! What is truth? I'll tell You: it's a word and nothing more. Poof! It's gone. If I were You, I'd save myself, fairy.

JOSHUA. I am saved, friend. Are you?

PILATE. You are arrogant.

PILATE'S WIFE. Have nothing to do with Him!

PILATE. *(To the crowd.)* I find in Him no fault but His damnable pride. But you have a custom that I should release one prisoner to you at Passover. Will you therefore that I release to you the queer or the thief, Barabbas?

ALL. Not the queer, the thief. Barabbas! Barabbas! Barabbas!

JUDAS. And Barabbas was released to them.

THADDEUS/BARRABAS. *(Kneeling before Pilate.)* God bless you, sir! I'll remember you for this. *(He kisses the hem of Pilate's robe, then stands.)* Then he got very drunk and went to a neighborhood they called Boys' Town and fucked his brains out — what was left of them.

JUDAS. "And the soldiers took Him to their company quarters and stripped Him and bound Him to a pillar and scourged Him while others knelt and adored Him as the King of the Queers." *(Dub Taylor, Spider Sloan and Billy Brown surround Joshua.)*

DUB TAYLOR. Hi, Joshua. Remember us? I'm Dub. He's Spider.

BILLY BROWN. And I'm Billy. *(During the following, Joshua is stripped, bound and scourged. It's theatricalized/stylized but it's never pretty. We should feel his passion.)*

BARTHOLOMEW/NUN. Now some of you, when you're bad, have been spanked at home by your mothers and fathers. And from time to time, here, at Christ the King School, I, too, have had to reprimand you, though lovingly, always very lovingly. Penny Williams, did you chew gum during Mass?

SIMON. Yes, Sister.

NUN. You know what to do. Put your hand out. No, knuckle-side up this time. This hurts me more than it hurts you. The good Lord did not invent straight rulers for such a purpose. Stop whimpering, Penny Williams. Take it like a man. Swat! But you know who it hurts even more than you or I? Jesus Christ, your Savior. That's who. Swat! He cries to Himself up in Heaven when He sees bad little girls like you chewing gum during the Holy Sacraments of His most holy Mass. Swat! Swat! Swat! Now, open your catechisms. Why did God make you, Timothy Sheahan.

JUDAS. "And the soldiers plaited a crown of thorns and put it on His head."

JAMES/LITTLE BOY. Sister Mary Margaret told us one of the thorns was so long it went right through His skull and came out in the middle of His right eye!

JUDAS. "They put Him in a purple robe and gave Him a stick as a scepter and mocked Him and smote Him with their hands again." *(Peter has been watching Joshua's torment in an agony of his own.)*

PETER. Don't hurt Him!

JAMES THE LESS/PHARISEE.   His name is Simon Peter. He's one of them, too!

PETER.   Don't be ridiculous.

MATTHEW/PHILISTINE.   I saw them dancing together at a club!

PETER.   I don't know what you're talking about.

JOHN/HYPOCRITE.   He corrupted my children.

PETER.   Do I look like one of them? I despise Him! *(He spits in Joshua's face.)*

JAMES.   Cock-a-doodle-do! *(Joshua just looks at Peter.)*

PETER.   I had no choice! They would have killed us all.

SIMON.   Cock-a-doodle-do!

PETER.   I'm Your rock. You said so Yourself. Someone has to spread the Word after You're ... *(He catches himself.)*

BARTHOLOMEW.   Cock-a-doodle-do!

PETER.   What would You have done?

ALL.   Crucify Him! Crucify Him.

JUDAS.   "And they took Jesus, Joshua, and led Him away." *(A cross is brought out from behind the stage. It is put on Joshua's shoulders. He falls under the weight of it.)*

JOHN/SIMON OF CYRENAE.   Let me help You, brother.

JOSHUA.   What is your name, brother?

SIMON OF CYRENAE.   Simon. Simon of Cyrenae. *(John carries the cross for Joshua through a jeering throng.)* Try not to stop. They'll only beat You harder.

JOSHUA.   I thought I saw My mother. There, in the distance. I was wrong. *(Mary waves to her son. He doesn't see her.)*

MARY.   That last night, when Mary was told her son would not receive her, she did not understand. Her life had not been an easy one. Who would take care of her in her old age? She was no longer beautiful. Now she looked away and lowered her head when His eyes sought hers.

JUDAS.   "And they came to the place called Golgotha. The place of skulls because so many criminals' bodies lay unburied there. The crowd grew silent. They stripped Him of His garment, which was of a color purple to mock His divinity."

THADDEUS.   I got dibs on the purple dress!

JUDAS.   "They lay Him roughly down on the cross."

JOSHUA. Oh!

JUDAS. "And then they nailed Him to it." *(Thaddeus strikes the first nail. Joshua screams in agony. Thaddeus drops the hammer.)*

MATTHEW. Idiot! *(He picks up the hammer and drives in the second nail.)*

JOHN AND JAMES THE LESS. *(Drop to their knees.)* Our Father who art in heaven.

MATTHEW. Shut them up! Will somebody shut them up!

JUDAS. "A third nail was driven into His feet." *(Matthew drives in the third nail. Someone in the crowd faints. Thunder and lightning. A wind begins to build.)*

MATTHEW. *(The Soldiers make ready to raise the cross.)* One, two, three, heave!! *(The cross is raised. For the first time we see how horribly Joshua has been battered. Blood runs down his face and body. His eyes are half-swollen shut. It should be hard to look at him.)* Blessed are the meek, for they shall ... what was that, cowboy?

JAMES THE LESS. Architect, what have you done?

JOSHUA. Father, forgive them: they know not what they do.

JUDAS. "In the distance, on the horizon, He could see some of the disciples who were too frightened to come closer and His mother and His aunt and the Mary called the Magdalene. It was some comfort."

JOHN. He looks thirsty. Give Him something to cool His parched mouth.

BARTHOLOMEW. Here You go, cowboy! A sponge soaked in vinegar.

THADDEUS. Suck on that!

JUDAS. "Two other criminals were put to death with Him. Crucified, one to each side." *(Simon and Andrew stand to each side of Joshua, their arms extended, as if they, too, were crucified.)*

ANDREW. Hey, faggot! If I was the Son of God I wouldn't be hanging here with my dick between my legs. Save us all if You're really Him.

SIMON. Don't listen to him.

ANDREW. You can't do it 'cause You're not! Fuck. *(He bows his head and dies.)*

SIMON. If You are the Son of God, remember me when You get to Heaven.

JOSHUA.   Brother, you shall be with Me in Paradise today.

SIMON.   I believe You, brother. *(He bows his head and dies. There is a crash of thunder and a flash of lightning. We hear the loud howling of the wind.)*

JUDAS.   "A savage darkness fell over the place. The earth shook and graves opened. The people fled in terror. What had they done?" *(He looks to Joshua.)* Are you suffering, Joshua?

JOSHUA.   Horribly, horribly. *(Joshua lets out a cry of agony.)* Eloi, Eloi, lama sabbacthani!

JUDAS.   Which is Hebrew and which means "My God, my God, why have You forsaken Me?"

GOD.   This is my Son with Whom I am well pleased.

JOSHUA.   Father, into Thy hands I commend My spirit. *(He dies. We hear three loud knocks. Judas takes up a piece of rope and looks at it. Gradually, the other Actors return to C.)*

THE ACTOR PLAYING JOHN.   Our play is over but the end is still to come. All these things you have seen and heard are the first birth pangs of the new age. Hold yourselves ready, therefore, because the son of Man will come at the time when you least expect Him.

THE ACTOR PLAYING JAMES THE LESS.   Look what they did to Him. Look what they did to Him.

THE ACTOR PLAYING JUDAS.   Sometimes I mourn for Judas, too. I believe Joshua would have.

THE ACTOR PLAYING THADDEUS.   Maybe other people have told His story better. Other actors. This was our way.

THE ACTOR PLAYING SIMON.   If we have offended, so be it.

THE ACTOR PLAYING BARTHOLOMEW.   He loved every one of us. That's all He was about.

THE ACTOR PLAYING JAMES THE LESS.   Look what they did to Him.

THE ACTOR PLAYING MATTHEW.   *(To us.)* Peace be with you.

THE ACTOR PLAYING PHILIP.   *(To us.)* Good-bye. Thank you. *(The Actors exit, making conversation, or not, as they go. One Actor remains. He kneels at the side of the cross. The house lights are turned up. The play is over.)*

THE END

PROPERTY LIST

Pitcher of water (JOHN)
Large basket with folded slips of paper (PHILIP)
Nails (ANDREW, THADDEUS)
Pieces of silver (JOHN)
Noose (JOHN)
Loaf of bread (THOMAS)
Rope (THADDEUS)
Crown of thorns (MATTHEW)
Souvenir ashtray (SIMON)
Fish (THOMAS)
Vinegar (BARTHOLOMEW)
Sponge (ANDREW)
Spear (THADDEUS)
Chalice (PETER)
Stuffed dog on wheels (SIMON)
Blue suede shoes (PETER)
Pink suede belt (SIMON)
Varsity letter (JAMES)
Picture of James Dean (MATTHEW)
Pack of Lucky Strike cigarettes (PETER)
Maxwell House coffee can (PETER)
Copy of *Old Testament* (JAMES)
Diary (BARTHOLOMEW)
Baby (doll) (PETER, MARY)
Cuban cigars (ROOM SERVICE #2)
Flexible Flyer (ROOM SERVICE #3)
Football
45 RPM record (MARY)
Towels
Envelope (BERT MOODY)
Belongings (JOSHUA)
Jukebox
Poppers (JUDAS)

Bag of coins (HIGH PRIEST)
Sword (PETER)
Bible (PHILIP)
Hammer (THADDEUS)

SOUND EFFECTS

Hammering
Cheering at a football game
Lovemaking
Fight sounds
Doors slamming
Roar of trucks
Crickets
Thunder
Wind